ESSENTIAL 101 TIPS

PUPPY CARE

D1009133

PUPPY CARE

Bruce Fogle, DVM

A DK PUBLISHING BOOK

Editor Simon Adams
Art Editor Alison Shackleton
Series Editor Gillian Roberts
Series Art Editor Clive Hayball
Production Controller Lauren Britton
US Editor Laaren Brown

First American Edition, 1997
2 4 6 8 10 9 7 5 3 1
Published in the United States by DK Publishing, Inc.
95 Madison Avenue, New York, New York 10016

Visit us on the World Wide Web at http://www.dk.com

Copyright © 1997 Dorling Kindersley Limited, London

A catalog record is available from the Library of Congress

ISBN 0–7894–1463–5

Text film output by The Right Type, Great Britain
Reproduced by Colourscan, Singapore
Printed and bound in Italy by Graphicom

ESSENTIAL TIPS

PAGES 8-12

CHOOSING A PUPPY

1 ....Why have a puppy?
2 ....Male or female?
3 ....Pedigree or mongrel?
4 ....Cross-breed?
5 ....A puppy or a dog?
6 ....Long coat or short?

PAGES 17-22

BUYING YOUR PUPPY

13 ....Where to buy?
14 ....When to buy?
15 ....Meet the parents
16 ....Visit the litter
17 ....What to look for
18 ....Making your choice
19 ....Health check
20 ....Your puppy & the law

PAGES 23-30

BRINGING YOUR PUPPY HOME

21 ....Prepare your home
22 ....Choice of bed
23 ....Use a puppy pen or crate
24 ....Meeting the family
25 ....Naming your puppy
26 ....Meeting other pets
27 ....Identify your puppy
28 ....First night at home
29 ....Collar your puppy
30 ....Types of leash
31 ....First toys

PAGES 13-16

YOUR NEWBORN PUPPY

7 ....After the birth
8 ....Monitor weight gain
9 ....Four weeks old
10 ....Handle daily
11 ....Eight weeks old
12 ....Weaning puppies

32...............Puppy-proof your yard
33 ....Toxic plants
34.......................Outdoor kennels

PAGES 31-41

FEEDING YOUR PUPPY

35 ....A balanced diet
36 ....Your growing puppy
37 ....You're in control!
38 ....Feeding guidelines
39 ....Food temperature
40..........................Waiting for food
41 ....Feeding equipment
42 ....Daily water
43..............................Canned foods
44 ....Add dry meal
45 ....Dry foods
46 ....Semimoist foods
47 ....Biscuits

48 ....Treats & tidbits
49...Chews
50 ....Fresh foods
51 ....Special meals
52 ....Fresh meat
53 ....Vegetarian food
54 ....Vitamin supplements

PAGES 42-47

GROOMING & CLEANING

55............Why groom your puppy?
56 ....Basic grooming equipment
57.............Grooming a smooth coat
58 ....Grooming a short coat
59 ....Grooming a long coat
60.................Grooming a silky coat
61 ....Inspect the eyes
62 ....Inspect the ears
63 ....Clip the nails
64...........................Clean the teeth
65 ....Bathing your puppy

PAGES 48-53

FIRST TRAINING

66 ....Train immediately
67 ....Call your puppy's name
68 ....Use praise
69 ....Reward your puppy
70 ....Just say no!
71 ....Acquiring basic social skills
72 ....Paper training
73 ....Toilet training outside
74 ....Clean up after your puppy
75 ....Introduce the leash
76 ....Meeting a stranger
77 ....Meeting other dogs
78 ....Leaving your puppy alone

PAGES 54-63

NEXT STEPS

79 ....Repeat the command
80 ....Come!
81 ....Come & sit!

82 ....Lie down!
83 ....Down!
84 ....Stay!
85 ....Jumping up
86 ....Chewing objects
87 ....Training more than one puppy
88 ....Heeling
89 ....Walking on the leash

PAGES 64-69

HEALTH & SAFETY

90 ....Vaccinate your puppy
91 ....Basic first aid kit
92 ....Basic bandaging
93 ....Giving liquid medicines
94 ....Swallowing pills
95 ....Prevent road accidents
96 ...How to remove foreign objects
97 ....Hypothermia
98 ....Chemical hazards
99 ....Electrical hazards
100 ....Avoid heatstroke
101 ....In the car

INDEX 70
ACKNOWLEDGMENTS 72

CHOOSING A PUPPY

1 WHY HAVE A PUPPY?

Owning a puppy is like having a new child in the house. It will become the focus of the family's affections, but will bring with it extra responsibilities for many years ahead. Make sure, therefore, that you select a breed that fits into your lifestyle, both now and in the future. The amount of exercise, food, grooming, and general attention your pet needs varies with its size and temperament. Size can be deceptive: some small dogs need more exercise than their much larger relatives.

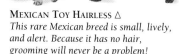

MEXICAN TOY HAIRLESS △
This rare Mexican breed is small, lively, and alert. Because it has no hair, grooming will never be a problem!

Coat is long, silky, and curly

KING CHARLES SPANIEL △
This small breed is obedient, affectionate, and is a suitable family pet.

LABRADOR RETRIEVER ▽
The Labrador Retriever's reputation as an amiable family dog is fully justified, but owners must be prepared to cope with its lively nature.

Short-haired Labradors shed their coat all year round

◁ **AMERICAN WATER SPANIEL**
Like other breeds of spaniel, the American Water Spaniel is a companionable dog that will be an attentive pet.

Hair is curly and will require plenty of attention

Puppy has well-defined markings

◁ **BERNESE MOUNTAIN DOG**
This large mountain dog is delightful, but its long coat will require plenty of grooming.

Coat is soft and silky with a good sheen

BERGAMASCO ▷
The Bergamasco sheepdog has a distinct, corded coat that will require constant grooming. This curious-looking dog is loyal and observant, and grows to medium height.

Triangular ears are hidden beneath hair

Hair forms long, wavy, strong locks

Facial hair has finer texture

Body is strong and well muscled

2 MALE OR FEMALE?

Deciding which sex of puppy to acquire is largely a matter of your own preference, but remember:
- Young unneutered males can be a nuisance when sexually excited.
- Bitches are often easier to train.
- Bitches go into "heat" twice a year, requiring extra vigilance.
- Owning a bitch means attention from male dogs and the possibility of unwanted pregnancies.

3 PEDIGREE OR MONGREL?

A pedigree or purebred puppy comes with documentation, just like a car, so you know what sort of puppy you are buying and what sort of temperament it may have. With a mongrel, or random-bred puppy, it is often difficult to foresee how it will behave, or even what size it will grow up to be.

▽ **MONGREL PUPPIES**
Mongrels are often in need of good homes and are particularly endearing.

PEDIGREE PUPPIES △
Purebred puppies can suffer from inherited diseases and disabilities.

4 CROSSBREED?

While mongrels can be a risk, pedigree puppies may cost a great deal. A satisfactory alternative is to buy a crossbreed – the offspring of two purebred dogs. A crossbred puppy is unlikely to develop many of the negative health or temperament aspects associated with its parents' pure breeding, and at best displays the most appealing characteristics of its common heritage.

◁ BEST OF BOTH WORLDS
A crossbred puppy, like this cross between a Border Terrier and a Jack Russell, often combines the best features of both parents.

5 A PUPPY OR A DOG?

When you buy a puppy, you are buying it for its whole life. You could be spending the next 14 years or longer with your pet. To start with, the puppy will take up many hours a day while you train, exercise, and just spend time with it. If you don't have lots of time and patience for a young pet, go for an adult dog instead. It should be housebroken already and therefore easier and less time-consuming to look after than a puppy.

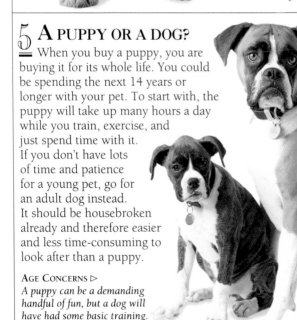

Trained adult dog behaves well and will sit quietly

AGE CONCERNS ▷
A puppy can be a demanding handful of fun, but a dog will have had some basic training.

6 LONG COAT OR SHORT?

When you are choosing a puppy, consider its type of coat carefully. A long-coated puppy, such as an Afghan Hound, needs daily combing and a regular trim, while a smooth, short-haired breed, such as a Dalmatian or Doberman, is much easier to maintain and needs only a weekly brushing. A puppy with wiry hair, such as an Airedale or Border Terrier, requires regular hand-stripping or clipping.

▽ SMOOTH COATS
The smooth coats of short-haired breeds, such as this Harrier mother and puppy, need little attention other than a weekly brushing.

Smooth coat offers little protection from cold weather

CURLY COATS
Puppies with curly coats that do not shed, such as the different breeds of poodle, must be clipped regularly – every two months – to keep them in good condition.

Paws and legs need special attention

LONG-HAIRED COATS ▽
Breeds with long coats, such as the Rough Collie or Old English Sheepdog, need daily grooming to prevent the coat from becoming matted.

Ears and eyes are hidden by long hair

Knots and tangles are common in long coats

Long coats offer protection from the cold

YOUR NEWBORN PUPPY

7 AFTER THE BIRTH

For the first three weeks of their lives, newborn puppies are completely dependent on their mother for food, warmth, and security. You can help the litter by making sure that they are kept warm and that their mother is well nourished, healthy, and producing sufficient milk. With extra-large litters, a mother's milk can sometimes be supplemented with special canine milk formula.

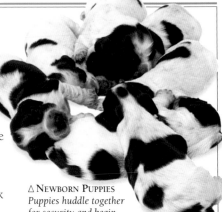

△ NEWBORN PUPPIES
*Puppies huddle together
for security and begin
to behave as a pack.*

△ BOTTLE FEEDING
*Feed milk formula initially every two hours
if the mother has rejected her litter or does
not have enough milk. Ask a vet for guidance
on the exact amounts to feed.*

△ CLEANING UP
*Handle all puppies frequently, but take care
not to upset their mother. Each puppy's eyes,
ears, and mouth should be checked daily and
cleaned when needed with moist cotton.*

8 MONITOR WEIGHT GAIN

Keep track of your puppies' weight gain by carefully weighing each member of the litter daily. Lack of weight gain means that you might have to intervene to help weaker puppies get their proper share of their mother's most productive teats.

▽ THE DAILY WEIGH
Weigh newborn puppies daily to check their weight.

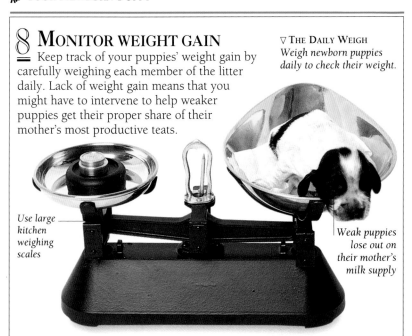

Use large kitchen weighing scales

Weak puppies lose out on their mother's milk supply

9 FOUR WEEKS OLD

Just as with small children, the environment in which a puppy is raised influences its behavior in adult life. This early period of socialization is very short, lasting for only a few months. During this period, puppies learn how to behave with other dogs and humans. At four weeks of age, a puppy's senses are well developed. A puppy should receive mental stimulation and learn how to behave with other dogs through regular play.

△ LIVING TOGETHER
If you have a litter of puppies, keep them in a large pen so that they can become adjusted to their surroundings without being frightened.

10 HANDLE DAILY

Begin to handle and groom your new puppy as soon as it is old enough to wander away from its mother. From four weeks old, handle it several times daily so that it learns to accept being picked up and held by humans in later life. Early obedience training now will lead to good habits later. If you teach your puppy to stand or sit for its meal now, it will do so naturally in adult life.

Puppy feels secure when you touch it

LOVING HANDS ▷
Accepting human contact is a vital lesson for your growing puppy.

11 EIGHT WEEKS OLD

By the time your puppy is eight weeks old, it will be ready to leave its mother. It must be vaccinated against infectious diseases such as parvovirus and distemper. Early mental and physical stimulation ensures that it is now an active and confident young dog, able to cope with its exciting new world, and used to being handled. Be sure to provide it with frequent, nutritious meals, necessary both for its growth and its overall health.

◁ YOUR YOUNG DOG
At eight weeks, your puppy is now a young dog. Its coat color will have changed to its adult pattern and markings.

12 WEANING PUPPIES

For the first three weeks of their lives, newborn puppies are totally dependent on their mother for food and security. As they age, puppies can be weaned away from their mother's milk and introduced to a more adult diet. By six weeks old, puppies are fully weaned.

Weaning puppies

Age	Type of food	Number of feeds daily
3 weeks old	Milky oatmeal or cereal, plus unlimited mother's milk	2 milky meals, plus normal feeding by mother
4 weeks old	Hard-boiled or scrambled egg yolk; milky cereal; ground meat or prepared puppy food; water & mother's milk	1 egg meal or 1 cereal meal; 1 ground meat or puppy food meal; normal feeding by mother
5 weeks old	Hard-boiled or scrambled egg yolk; milky cereal; ground meat or prepared puppy food; water & mother's milk	1 egg meal or 1 cereal meal; 4 ground meat or puppy food meals; normal feeding by mother
6 weeks old	Ground, cooked meat or prepared puppy food & dry food; egg; cereal; milk if tolerated, as mother's milk is drying up	4 meat & dry food meals; 1 egg or cereal meal if puppy will eat it; cow's milk & water
7 weeks old	Increased amounts of meat & dry food; freely available water; milk if tolerated as mother is now dry; egg; cereal	4 meat & dry food meals; 1 egg or cereal meal if puppy will eat it; cow's milk & water
8 weeks old	Increased amounts of meat & dry food; freely available water; cow's milk	4 meat & dry food meals; cow's milk & water

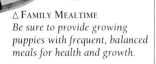

△ FAMILY MEALTIME
Be sure to provide growing puppies with frequent, balanced meals for health and growth.

BUYING YOUR PUPPY

Check the health and condition of each puppy carefully

Reputable breeder will ensure puppy is in good health

13 WHERE TO BUY?

The best place to buy your new puppy is from a reputable breeder. Avoid puppy farms or mills, as they often provide inhumane conditions for mothers and give little attention to the puppies' health. Be wary of pet shops – they can sometimes be fertile environments for a range of infectious diseases, and may supply you with an unhealthy individual purchased from a puppy farm.

△ TAKE YOUR TIME
All puppies look appealing, but control your impulse to buy the first puppy that catches your eye. It may be the best, but you can only be sure after seeing a number of puppies.

ANIMAL SHELTERS
Animal shelters always have a surplus of puppies requiring homes. The best shelters interview you before letting you take home one of their charges. Because these puppies had previous homes, be prepared for behavioral problems. Such puppies take time to settle down.

14 WHEN TO BUY?

The best age for a puppy to leave its mother and enter your home is at about eight weeks. Puppies younger than this are not fully weaned and still rely on their mother for protection and support. Puppies over about 12 weeks of age may have already formed unwanted habits and may find it difficult to adapt to a new home. At eight weeks, a puppy is independent, but still young enough for you to train it properly for adult life.

READY FOR A NEW HOME ▷
At about eight weeks, your new puppy is ready to leave its mother and move into your home.

15 MEET THE PARENTS

Responsible breeders are proud of their stock and will be happy to introduce you to the litter's mother and also the father, if available. The parents' appearance and behavior will give you some idea of your puppy's mature size and likely temperament. Beware of individuals who are unable to show you the mother: they may not be genuine breeders but agents for disreputable puppy mills.

MEETING MOTHER ▷
Meeting the mother will tell you plenty about the likely temperament and behavior of your puppy.

Mother is placid and content

Puppies are well fed and cared for

16 VISIT THE LITTER

When visiting a litter, observe how the puppies behave together. Some may be retiring, others more bossy. Bear in mind that a very assertive, outgoing puppy often develops into a dominant adult and can be more difficult to train, while a shy, retiring puppy may grow up to be an insecure or fearful adult, a fairly common occurrence in some breeds, such as German Shepherds. Apart from considering temperament, decide which sex you prefer, and then select a bright, healthy puppy that seems to have the character you desire.

THE RIGHT CHOICE ▽
Visit the litter and carefully watch each puppy before you make a choice as to which one to buy.

Confident puppy enjoys being handled

THE ONE FOR YOU ▷
In the end, your choice of puppy will be just a matter of personal preference.

△ LOOK AT ALL THE PUPPIES
When buying a puppy, it is important to view the entire litter to see how each puppy behaves with its brothers and sisters.

17 WHAT TO LOOK FOR

Because of advances in nutrition, preventive medicine, and the treatment of diseases such as cancer, it is likely that you will share the next 14 years with your dog. So choose one that is not only right for your lifestyle today, but also one you think will still fit into your daily routine in ten years' time. Choose a puppy that appears bright, alert, and healthy. A reputable breeder will let you select a puppy conditional upon a vet examining it and certifying that it is healthy and strong.

Facial expression is quizzical but relaxed

Fur is shiny and soft, and feels clean and smooth

ELEVEN-WEEK-OLD PUPPY ▷
This Boxer puppy is inquisitive and alert. When it meets new people, it comes forward to investigate, which is a good sign of confidence. Puppies that are too confident can develop into dominant adults.

Muscles are well developed and symmetrical

MOTHER'S CARE
A puppy should remain with its mother for at least eight weeks before it is ready to face life on its own. It is then at an ideal age to be trained.

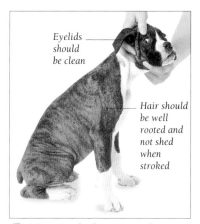

Eyelids should be clean

Hair should be well rooted and not shed when stroked

1 △ Examine both eyes to make sure they are clear and bright, and free from any discharge or redness. There should be good pigmentation, and no sign of any inflammation or irritation.

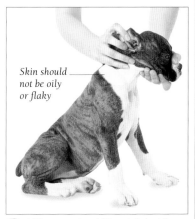

Skin should not be oily or flaky

2 △ The ears should be pink inside with neither an unpleasant odor nor any sign of crusty or waxy discharge, which may indicate ear mites. Check that the ear-flaps hang evenly.

Gently part lips to inspect teeth and gums

Hairless skin should be pink and unstained

3 △ The gums should be odor free and pink. Except in certain breeds, such as this Boxer, the teeth need to meet perfectly in a scissor bite.

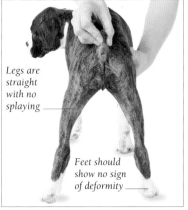

Legs are straight with no splaying

Feet should show no sign of deformity

4 △ The anal region ought to be clean and dry. There should be no inflammation or sign of diarrhea, or any discharge from the genital area.

18 MAKING YOUR CHOICE

When handling your prospective puppy, always support its hindquarters. The puppy should feel firm and quite heavy. Ask to see the parents' registration documents and health certificates, verifying the absence of any hereditary conditions. Ultimately, your decision on which puppy to own will rest on your puppy's looks and its unique, endearing behavior.

Healthy puppy feels solid and surprisingly heavy

YOUR UNIQUE PUPPY ▷
Every puppy has its own special personality and way of behaving.

Your vet will soon get to know your new puppy

19 HEALTH CHECK

As soon as you obtain your new puppy, take it to the vet for a health check. Choose your vet with the help of pet-owning friends, and visit the office first to see if the practice suits your needs. Most vets provide 24-hour emergency care. Find out the location of your local emergency facilities and keep the telephone number close at hand. Veterinary treatment can be expensive, but insurance will help cover some costs.

20 YOUR PUPPY AND THE LAW

Following public concern, it is an offense in many countries to allow a dog to be dangerously out of control in a public place. You must always obey local muzzling laws, but use only a safe, basket-type muzzle that allows your puppy to pant freely. Your vet will advise you on any local regulations. If you have any doubts about your puppy's temperament, it is safest to keep it muzzled in public.

BRINGING YOUR PUPPY HOME

21 PREPARE YOUR HOME

You will need to prepare your home carefully before your new puppy arrives. A puppy is naturally inquisitive and will want to smell and chew any new objects it finds.

- Check all electrical appliances for dangling cords.
- Place all cleaning and decorating materials out of reach.
- Remove valuable or sentimental objects until your puppy is past the chewing stage.
- Keep outside doors latched and low windows closed.

△ TRANSPORTING YOUR PUPPY
Use a specially-made pet carrier to bring your puppy home.

◁ HOME COMFORTS
To help your puppy feel warm and secure at night, wrap a hot-water bottle in its blanket. Do not place the bottle next to its skin.

ONE ROOM AT A TIME
Your new puppy will be disoriented when you bring it home. Restrict it to a single room and let it explore its new home slowly.

23

22 CHOICE OF BED

Buy your puppy a bed of its own before you bring it home. Beanbag beds are colorful, but you may prefer to buy a wicker or a semi-indestructible plastic basket.

WICKER OR PLASTIC? ▷
Wicker baskets look good, but chew-proof plastic is easy to clean and hard to damage.

△ **BEANBAG BED**
Form-fitting bean-bags make ideal beds. They are light, soft, retain body heat, and are easy to wash. Most puppies enjoy the security they feel when asleep on one.

23 USE A PUPPY PEN OR CRATE

As soon as you arrive home with your new puppy, introduce it to its own den – either a four-sided pen or a metal-grilled crate. Line the den with soft bedding. Make sure it is inviting by placing food treats or toys inside. A pen or crate offers security to your puppy.

Pen is open at top so puppy can be removed

Puppy can watch household activity

Newspaper will soak up any accidents

Make sure fresh water is always available

24 MEETING THE FAMILY

It is important for you to introduce your new puppy to your family in the correct way. Your puppy is a member of the family now and must be treated with equal respect. Even a friendly puppy should be introduced to young children in the presence, and under the supervision, of an adult. While your puppy may enjoy being petted by adults, it might not be used to the rapid movements of children.

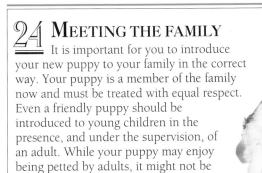

A CHILD'S HELP ▷
Young children enjoy feeding and caring for a new family member.

SHARING TASKS
Even young children can help care for the family pet. By choosing a fun task, such as grooming, feeding, or walking (at all times under adult supervision), children develop a close relationship with their new pet.

25 NAMING YOUR PUPPY

One of the first things you must do with your new puppy is to give it a name. Remember: the name you choose will be with your pet for its entire life, and you will have to use it every day – in the home, out in the park, or on the street. The best names are short ones. Have the name engraved on your puppy's ID tag.

26 MEETING OTHER PETS

An older, well-established resident dog may resent the arrival of a new puppy, so it is important to supervise their first few meetings. Allow your dog to investigate the puppy when it is asleep. Securing your puppy inside a pen or crate allows the resident dog to investigate its new companion without harassing it.

Tail rises in anticipation

THE FAMILY DOG ▷
Given time, your dog will learn to accept its new housemate.

△ **CAT & DOG**
Cats and dogs can live peacefully together and enjoy each other's company if their first introductions are not threatening.

Dog is calm and placid

27 IDENTIFY YOUR PUPPY

It is important to tag your puppy so that if it gets lost, it can be returned to you. Engraved or tube tags carry vital information about your puppy, including its name, your own telephone number and address, and possibly the address of your vet too.

△ TUBE TAG   △ STEEL TAG   △ BRASS TAG

PUPPY SCAN
Your vet can insert a tiny microchip under the skin on the puppy's neck. Information on this chip can be read using a handheld scanner.

28 FIRST NIGHT AT HOME

The first night that your puppy is away from its brothers and sisters in new surroundings is always the most difficult. Provide it with a chewable toy for comfort and, if you are willing, place its den in your bedroom so that it is reassured by your presence. With a little perseverance, your puppy will soon settle down.

1 △ Make the den inviting by placing food treats or toys inside. Initially, leave the door open to allow your puppy to wander in and out as it pleases.

2 △ At night, do not respond to any plaintive cries your puppy makes, or you will unwittingly train your puppy to whine for attention.

◁ SWEET DREAMS
At first your puppy will need to sleep in your bedroom. As it gets older, it should happily accept sleeping elsewhere.

ALARM CALL
For the first few weeks, you will need to set your alarm during the night to take your puppy outside to relieve itself.

29 COLLAR YOUR PUPPY

When you get your puppy, provide it with a collar and leash and attach any identification tag. It is important to get a puppy used to wearing a collar from as young as eight weeks of age. Start by putting the collar on the puppy for short periods each day. Make sure that the collar sits comfortably and is not too tight. Always remove the collar when the puppy is unsupervised.

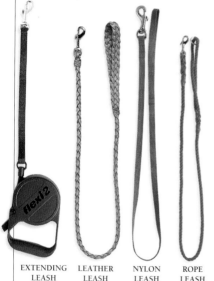

NO CHOKE CHAINS
Do not use a choke chain as it could restrict your puppy's windpipe. Choke chains are only for adult dogs insensitive to touch or with thick fur.

30 TYPES OF LEASH

Leashes and collars are usually made of leather, nylon, or rope, and vary considerably in quality, price, and usefulness. Braided or rolled leather can be expensive, but is comfortable and long lasting. Nylon is firm, supple, and usually cheaper. An extending leash is practical because it allows your puppy more freedom than an ordinary leash, while you – the owner – still retain control.

HARNESSES & HALTERS
Harnesses and halters can be useful for some adult dogs. A light harness is suitable for small dogs, while a head halter controls strong dogs.

EXTENDING LEASH   LEATHER LEASH   NYLON LEASH   ROPE LEASH

31 FIRST TOYS

Well-designed toys help stimulate your puppy physically and mentally. Your puppy will love toys with a distinctive odor and ones that are fun to chew, chase, and retrieve. Maintain your puppy's interest in a toy by limiting access to special times only, such as periods alone in its den, when the toy will act as a distraction. Give toys selectively as a prize for good behavior, and put them away after use so that your puppy knows they belong to you.

△ **CHEWY BONE**
Gnawing on a nylon bone exercises the jaws and cleans the teeth.

△ **DOG PULL**
Only use a tug-of-war toy like this with a puppy that willingly gives it up when you command it to do so.

CHEWY TOY ▷
This rubber toy is chewable and also bounces erratically when it is thrown, stimulating a puppy to chase it.

◁ **SQUEAKY TOY**
This plastic die squeaks when chewed, appealing to your puppy's basic hunting instincts.

TOY TIME ▷
Playing with toys will exercise your puppy both mentally and physically. Toys can be used as both a reward and a comfort.

SAFETY FIRST
Take special care with squeaky toys: some curious puppies will try to eat the squeak. Small toys should be avoided; they can be easily swallowed.

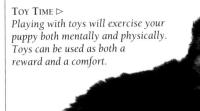

Plastic bones keep teeth and gums healthy

32 PUPPY-PROOF YOUR YARD

The greatest danger for your puppy in a yard is that it might escape. Use sturdy fences, latches, and gates. Make sure there are no gaps in the hedges, and place fine wire mesh at ground level on gates and beneath hedges to keep in small dogs. Make sure all tools are locked away, and put your trash bags in a covered container.

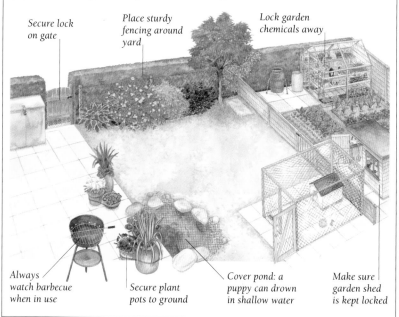

Secure lock on gate

Place sturdy fencing around yard

Lock garden chemicals away

Always watch barbecue when in use

Secure plant pots to ground

Cover pond: a puppy can drown in shallow water

Make sure garden shed is kept locked

33 TOXIC PLANTS

Many garden plants are poisonous to puppies. In particular they should be prevented from eating all kinds of fungi and kept away from laburnum trees and mistletoe berries. Keep plant bulbs such as daffodils out of reach. Yew, ivy, and lupine are also dangerous.

34 OUTDOOR KENNELS

When trained from an early age, most mature puppies are content to be housed in an outdoor kennel. It should contain bowls of food and water, and a few chewable toys. Never leave your puppy alone in a kennel for an extended period.

FEEDING YOUR PUPPY

35 A BALANCED DIET

Each puppy has its own individual dietary needs, which change at various stages of its life. Dogs cannot exist on meat alone since they are not true carnivores. Meat, which provides both protein and fat, should therefore never form more than half a puppy's diet. The rest of its daily calories need to come from carbohydrates, such as dog meal. Extra vitamins are not required if the diet is well balanced.

▽ FOOD FOR HEALTH
With a good diet, your puppy will grow up fit and strong.

Protein is needed for growth, tissue repair, and maintenance of vital body functions

Essential fatty acids give coat a handsome, glossy sheen

Carbohydrates add bulk to diet and help maintain regular bowel movement

36 YOUR GROWING PUPPY

Puppies need plenty of nutrients for healthy growth; each puppy also has its own specific nutritional needs. The chart below is an approximate guide only. If you are uncertain of what is best for your growing puppy, consult your vet.

A HUNGRY PUPPY △

DO NOT DISTURB! ▷
Avoid interrupting your puppy while it eats, or it will become nervous at feeding time.

Give your puppy food from a non-slip bowl, for easier eating

Daily calorie requirements

Type of dog	Calories needed at 2 months	Calories needed at 3 months	Calories needed at 6 months
Very small, e.g., Yorkshire Terrier	225	255	250
Small, e.g., Miniature Poodle	395	495	640
Medium, e.g., Standard Dachshund	535	770	980
Large, e.g., Standard Poodle	980	1,470	1,875
Giant, e.g., Rottweiler	1,220	1,935	2,870

37 YOU'RE IN CONTROL!

Some puppies are very fussy about what they eat and blackmail their owners into offering them their favorite foods. Be tough: your puppy should eat only what you want to feed it. The war of wills between you can be very frustrating, but eventually your puppy will eat whatever it is given.

LEADER OF THE PACK ▷
As much as you love your puppy, you must establish who's the boss in your own home!

38 FEEDING GUIDELINES

There are certain guidelines you need to observe when feeding your puppy. Follow them, and your puppy will develop into a healthy adult dog.

- Provide prepared food only from a reputable manufacturer.
- Dispose of any canned or moist food left uneaten.
- Discard leftover dry food at the end of each day.
- Never feed your puppy chicken or fish bones.
- Never feed cat food to a puppy: it's too high in protein.
- Never offer spoiled or stale food.
- If your puppy does not eat for 24 hours, consult a vet.

SHARING FOOD
Although some puppies in the same household may be happy to eat together, always provide separate bowls.

◁ HEALTH FIRST
Follow the rules of feeding, and your puppy will receive a healthy and safe diet.

39 FOOD TEMPERATURE

When feeding your puppy, make sure that you serve its food at room temperature. Do not serve food that is taken straight from the refrigerator or dish up cooked food that is still hot from the oven. Your puppy's mouth is sensitive to extremes of cold and heat and could be harmed if it eats food that is too cold or hot. If in doubt, let any food stand for a few minutes before serving.

△ SAFE EATING
For your puppy's safety, serve its food barely warm.

40 WAITING FOR FOOD

Unless properly trained, puppies have a tendency to beg shamelessly for food, especially for tidbits when you are eating. Establish a set routine for its mealtimes to prevent this, and offer your puppy food only in its own bowl. Teach your puppy to sit and wait in the presence of food, and to eat only when allowed to do so.

Puppy begs pleadingly for food

△ NO BEGGING
If you give in to your puppy when it begs for food, you will reinforce this behavior and soon have an overweight dog.

41 FEEDING EQUIPMENT

Your puppy should have its own food bowl, made of either heavy ceramic or stainless steel, rimmed with rubber to stop it from sliding. If you cook fresh meat for your puppy, use any saucepan you choose. As a hygiene precaution, keep all utensils separate from other kitchen equipment. Wash all bowls and cutlery after each meal.

△ PUPPY BOWL

△ PLASTIC LIDS

CAN OPENER △

△ SAUCEPAN

△ SPOON, FORK, & KNIFE

△ HEALTHY FEEDING
In the interests of hygiene, wash all bowls and equipment used after each meal. Cover partly used cans of food with plastic lids and store in the refrigerator, for three days at most.

42 DAILY WATER

A puppy loses water in urine and feces, through panting, and a little through sweat. Although canned food is usually three-quarters liquid, this is not enough to satisfy your pet's need for fluid. Fill its bowl with fresh water to the same level each day. If you notice that it is drinking more than usual, contact a vet, since this may indicate an internal disorder.

△ CERAMIC WATER BOWL

43 CANNED FOODS

Moist, meaty canned dog foods come in a wide variety of flavors and textures to suit your puppy's appetite and choice. Read the label on the can carefully to make sure you are buying the right one. Canned food is high in protein and can be mixed with dry dog meal to form a balanced diet. Canned foods are nutritious and tasty but will not stay fresh in the bowl for more than a few hours, so remove the bowl after feeding time.

△ MEATY CHUNKS

DRY DOG MEAL ▽

44 ADD DRY MEAL

Add dry dog meal to your puppy's canned food to ensure a balanced diet. Dry dog meal is an excellent source of fat, carbohydrates, and calories, and will exercise your puppy's jaws. When added to canned food, the crunchy meal improves the texture of the soft meat. Add the meal sparingly at first, increasing the amount according to preference.

45 DRY FOODS

Complete dry foods are well balanced and convenient to store in bulk. They are concentrated (with about four times the calories of canned foods), so a puppy needs smaller quantities. Buy dry foods made especially for puppies, since these are easily digested and have all the nutrients to sustain your puppy's growth.

PUPPY VARIETY ▷

46 SEMIMOIST FOODS

Complete semimoist foods are packaged in many flavors, including fish and cheese, and have three times the number of calories of canned foods. Like dry foods, they can be left out all day, so your puppy can eat them at its own pace. This form of pet food is less common than either moist or complete dry foods.

△ COMPLETE SEMIMOIST FOOD

47 BISCUITS

Dog biscuits are high in both fat and carbohydrate. By weight they contain as many calories as complete semimoist foods. Remember to include these calories when calculating your puppy's daily needs.

△ BACON FLAVORED

△ ASSORTED FLAVORS

△ CHEESE FLAVORED

△ MIXED FLAVORS

△ WHOLE-GRAIN

△ MARROWBONE

BISCUIT TREATS
It is good to give your puppy biscuits, but they are high in calories and could lead to obesity in later life. The more you give, the smaller the regular meals should be.

48 TREATS & TIDBITS

It is fun to give your puppy snack foods, but remember that they are high in calories and must be included in any daily calorie count. Offer your puppy treats and tidbits as part of a daily training regimen or as a reward for good behavior – not on demand – and limit the amount you give your puppy daily. Too many treats and tidbits and too little exercise will result in excess weight gain.

△ CHICKEN STRIPS   △ BEEF BONES   △ BEEF SOFT CHUNKS   △ SAVORY RINGS

49 CHEWS

Your growing puppy needs hard chews to exercise its teeth and gums, which is necessary for good dental hygiene. Chews contain few calories and are better than bones, which can fracture teeth or may splinter. You can buy chews in any good pet shop, but avoid small ones that may be easily swallowed. Encourage your puppy to play with its own chews rather than with your shoes or your favorite rug!

△ BONE CHEW   △ BALL CHEW   △ SHOE CHEW

△ CHEW STRIPS   △ HAMBURGER CHEW   △ PRETZEL CHEW

50 FRESH FOODS

Puppies are not complete carnivores and cannot live on meat alone. As a rule of thumb, foods that are balanced for humans are probably balanced for your pet. If you plan to feed your puppy fresh foods, make sure you provide it with all the nutritional building blocks it needs for its growing body. Mix meat or vegetable protein with vegetables, pasta, rice, cereals, or other foods to provide all the protein, fat, carbohydrate, vitamins, and minerals necessary for good health. Uncooked fruits and vegetables, such as apples, carrots, and cabbage, are good sources of additional vitamins.

△ MEAT & VEGETABLES
Meat and vegetables provide your puppy with almost all the ingredients it needs for a balanced diet.

△ GROUND MEAT
The high level of fat in ground meat provides a major source of calories for your puppy.

△ SCRAMBLED EGG
Light and nutritious, scrambled egg is ideal for puppies recovering from any type of illness.

△ PASTA
Pasta, although a good source of carbohydrates, is rather tasteless and needs some extra flavoring.

△ HEART
Because of its fat content, heart has twice as many calories as other organs, so feed only in moderation.

△ LIVER
Liver has a low calcium content, but is high in phosphorus and rich in vitamins A and B1.

51 SPECIAL MEALS

If your puppy is sick or convalescing, you will need to feed it with different foods. Chicken, fish, and rice are ideal choices if your puppy has a delicate stomach, while breakfast cereal with milk provides a tasty light meal that is rich in vitamins. Feed scrambled egg at times when your puppy is recovering from an illness.

△ CHICKEN
Chicken and turkey are easily digested and are low in calories.

△ FISH
Remove even the smallest bones before feeding fish to your puppy.

△ RICE
Boiled rice is very easily digested. Add to chicken if your puppy is recuperating.

52 FRESH MEAT

Your puppy will enjoy eating fresh meat, but remember that the nutrient content of fresh meat varies quite considerably, so keeping a consistently balanced diet can be quite difficult. You will need, therefore, to mix the meat with the correct amount of cereals, vegetables, pasta, and rice to ensure a properly balanced diet.

Analysis of fresh meats

Meats	Moisture	Protein	Fat	Calories per 100g
Tripe	88%	9%	3%	63 calories
Kidney	80%	16%	2.6%	86 calories
Chicken	74%	20%	4.3%	121 calories
Beef	74%	20%	4.6%	123 calories
Pork	72%	20%	7.1%	147 calories
Lamb	70%	20%	8.8%	162 calories
Heart	70%	14%	15.5%	197 calories

53 VEGETARIAN FOOD

Unlike cats, dogs are not true carnivores. They can survive on a vegetarian diet because they convert vegetable protein and fat into the ingredients necessary for all their body functions. Choose freshly cooked vegetables, such as cabbage and potatoes, as part of a balanced diet. Consult a vet if you wish to feed your puppy on a vegetarian diet, as it is harder to maintain balanced nutrition.

△ FRESH VEGETABLES
Potatoes, cabbage, and carrots are ideal vitamin-rich vegetarian dog foods.

◁ TOFU
Tofu (soy bean curd) is high in protein and low in calories and fat.

Puppy can convert vegetable protein and fat into nutrients

ADDED VITAMINS ▷
Raw vegetables and fruit are good sources of extra vitamins.

Raw carrot provides a tasty snack

54 VITAMIN SUPPLEMENTS

Your puppy should obtain all the vitamins and minerals it needs from a balanced diet. It may need supplements, however, as it grows into adulthood or when recovering from an illness. Rapidly developing puppies often need additional calcium, which can be obtained from tablets or from sterilized bonemeal. You should only give supplements under a vet's supervision, since too many can be as harmful as too few.

VITAMIN PILLS

GROOMING & CLEANING

55 WHY GROOM YOUR PUPPY?

Regularly groom your puppy to keep its skin, coat, teeth, gums, and nails in a healthy state. In this way, you are constantly reasserting your authority over your pet. Make the daily or weekly session a ritual that both you and your puppy enjoy and respect.

◁ REGULAR GROOMING
Groom your puppy's coat according to its length and texture. Ears, eyes, and teeth should be inspected once a week.

56 BASIC GROOMING EQUIPMENT

The basic equipment you need to groom your puppy consists of a brush and comb. The type of brush you buy depends on the length and type of your puppy's coat. For some breeds, scissors, a chamois leather cloth, and a set of electric clippers are also required.

Steel pins remove tangles

Bristles pick up dead hairs and dirt in coat

△ SLICKER BRUSH
Use a slicker brush to remove tangles from your puppy's coat.

△ BRISTLE BRUSH
Use a bristle brush to remove any dead hairs and to shine the coat.

△ COMB
Use a wide-toothed steel comb to straighten or part long hair.

57 GROOMING A SMOOTH COAT

Smooth-coated puppies do not need a lot of grooming, but they should have a regular brushing once or twice a week. Use a rubber brush to loosen any dead hair and surface dirt. Then remove dead hair and skin with a bristle brush. A coat conditioner can be applied at this stage to give the coat a glossy sheen. Finally, briskly polish the coat with a chamois cloth to bring out its natural shine.

Be careful of ears and eyes

△ RUBBER BRUSH

△ CHAMOIS LEATHER

△ LOOKING GOOD
Puppies with smooth coats are the easiest to groom and look immaculate with regular care and attention.

58 GROOMING A SHORT COAT

A puppy with a short coat must be groomed regularly to prevent matts. Use a slicker brush to remove any tangles, then brush thoroughly with a bristle brush to remove any dead hair and remaining dirt. Finally, run a fine comb through the feathers on the puppy's legs and tail. Trim any untidy hairs with a pair of scissors.

◁ SKIN CARE
While brushing your puppy's coat, check for any skin disorders or signs of parasites.

▽ **HANDLE WITH CARE**
When grooming a long coat, be careful not to pull out the hair or cause pain by vigorous brushing.

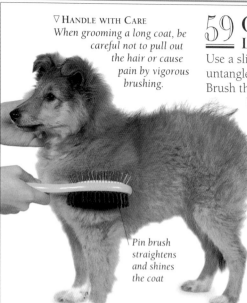

Pin brush straightens and shines the coat

59 GROOMING A LONG COAT

Use a slicker brush to gently untangle any matted hair or knots. Brush the coat again with a pin brush: you should feel no resistance as you brush through the coat. Then comb the hair with a wide-toothed comb, paying particular attention to the feathers on the legs. Finally, trim any long hairs around the legs and feet.

△ **WIDE-TOOTHED COMB**

60 GROOMING A SILKY COAT

Use a slicker brush to remove any tangles. Mats can be gently teased out. Brush the coat once more, using a bristle brush to bring out the shine. Part the long hair on the back, and comb each side straight down. Any untidy ends can be carefully trimmed with scissors. Trim around the ears, eyes, and feet.

NATURAL SHINE ▷
Use a bristle brush to enhance the natural shine of a silky coat. There should be no resistance to the brush.

61 INSPECT THE EYES

A puppy's eyes should be bright, clear, and free from any discharge, inflammation, or cloudiness. Remove mucus or debris from around the eye using a fresh piece of moistened cotton for each eye. If your puppy has watery eyes, blinks excessively, or has a discharge from the eye, seek your vet's advice.

EYE CHECK ▷
Examine your puppy's eyes at least once a week to make sure they are healthy.

PINK EARS ▽
Your puppy's ears should be dull pink inside.

62 INSPECT THE EARS

When cleaning your puppy's ears, check carefully for wax, odor, inflammation, and foreign material such as grass seeds. Hold open the ear with one hand; with the other, gently clean inside with a small piece of damp cotton or tissue. Use a fresh piece for each ear. Do not use a cotton swab because it can act like a plunger and push wax farther in.

63 CLIP THE NAILS

If you need to trim your puppy's nails, command it to sit. Spread each foot and inspect the area between the toes. Clean away any dirt with damp cotton. Clip each nail carefully; smooth rough edges with an emery board.

64 CLEAN THE TEETH

Check your puppy's teeth and gums once a week. Make sure there is no sign of gum infection or tartar buildup on the teeth. Gently brush the teeth and gums with a soft toothbrush, using either diluted salt water or a canine toothpaste.

65 BATHING YOUR PUPPY

Routine grooming keeps a puppy's coat in a healthy condition, but bathing is sometimes necessary if your puppy gets very dirty or smelly, or if you need to treat the condition of its skin. Rinse your puppy well, as residual shampoo in its coat can irritate the skin and cause scratching.

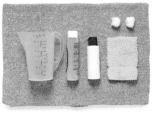

△ BATHING EQUIPMENT

1 △ Brush your puppy. Plug its ears with cotton. Stand it in the bath on a rubber mat. Hold it tightly by the collar and pour warm water over it.

Be careful not to splash soap into eyes

2 △ Using a canine shampoo, soap your puppy all over except for its head. Hold it firmly. Work up a lather, massaging against the lie of the coat.

3 △ Lather the puppy's head with a tearless shampoo poured in your hands. Massage its hair gently, being careful to avoid the mouth and eyes.

Use warm water to rinse hair

4 △ Rinse the head first before rinsing the rest of the body. This will stop it from shaking water all over the place. Take care to remove all shampoo.

Use a clean, dry towel to dry head

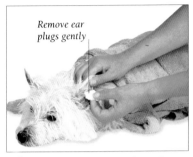

Remove ear plugs gently

5 △ If needed, rub conditioner into the coat only. Then rinse the head again, followed by the rest of the body.

6 △ Squeeze excess water from the coat, then dry thoroughly with a large towel. Remove the ear plugs and dry the inside of each ear.

Brush hair straight, away from body

SKIN CARE
Bathing can help eliminate certain skin parasites and treat a variety of dry and oily skin conditions. A vet might suggest you use medically therapeutic shampoos. If so, follow the manufacturer's instructions.

7 △ Use a hair dryer set on warm, not hot, on puppies with healthy skin, but not on those prone to itchiness.

AFTER A BATH ▷
Make sure your puppy does not roll over to cover itself in more natural smells!

FIRST TRAINING

66 TRAIN IMMEDIATELY

You must begin to train your puppy as soon as you bring it home. Your puppy relies on you to help it learn from an early age so that it grows up to be a trusting, even-tempered, sociable animal, at ease with other dogs and with humans. When your puppy is eight weeks old, you can begin gentle training for obedience and hygiene. But remember: some puppies are easier to train than others because of their different temperaments, so be patient.

START NOW ▷
It is never too early to begin to train your puppy to be obedient and hygienic.

NAME CALLING ▷
The first step in effective puppy training is to get your puppy to respond to its own name.

67 CALL YOUR PUPPY'S NAME

Each time you train or play with your puppy, speak its name repeatedly. A sharp, two-syllable name – like Sparky or Rover – is easiest for a puppy to learn. After a time, your puppy will recognize its name and will stop and listen to you when you use it. Once you have gained your puppy's attention in this way, you can then begin to train it to obey a series of basic commands.

Puppies, like children, respond well to praise

68 USE PRAISE

Always praise your puppy during training. Even a very young puppy is sensitive to the manner and tone of your voice, and will understand when you are genuinely pleased with its behavior. Your puppy will quickly learn what words of praise, such as "good dog," mean. Enthusiastic words of praise should always accompany other types of reward.

◁ **PRAISEWORTHY**
Your puppy knows it has done well when it hears praise in your voice.

Puppy sits obediently when praised

69 REWARD YOUR PUPPY

Words are not the only way in which you can reward your puppy when it has done well. Praise your puppy's good conduct with a friendly stroke or two. You can also reward your puppy with low-calorie food treats and snacks, or award it a prize of an exciting new toy for good behavior. But be sure to combine all rewards with verbal praise.

Favorite foods are useful as rewards for good behavior

Stroke your puppy's chin to indicate your praise

◁ **PLENTY OF REWARDS**
Physical attention, food treats, and toys can all be used in training to reward your puppy for behaving well.

70 JUST SAY NO!

One of the first words your puppy must understand is "No." With this single word, you remain in control, and accidents are prevented. Just as you use a friendly voice and warm body language to reward, adopt a stern tone and a dominant stance when issuing a reprimand. There is no need to shout, as most puppies are all too eager to please you.

◁ QUIET CONTROL
There is no need to shout or even raise your voice to assert your authority.

71 ACQUIRING BASIC SOCIAL SKILLS

A puppy's ability to learn is at its greatest during its first three months. If your puppy is denied regular social contact with other dogs during this important stage, it may not develop the social skills necessary for meeting strange dogs later in life. Some vets even organize puppy parties for single pets!

Puppy feels secure enough to join in the fun

△ SOCIAL CONTROL
By meeting other puppies at an early age, your puppy will be better prepared for adult life.

Friendly play helps your puppy make friends easily

72 PAPER TRAINING

When your puppy puts its nose down and sniffs, it usually signifies that it wishes to relieve itself. Be prepared to place your puppy quickly on sheets of newspaper. It is pointless to punish accidents, but if you catch your puppy in the act, sternly say "No" to teach it that the paper must be used.

Praise your puppy when it uses the newspaper

THE NEED FOR TRAINING ▷
Puppies relieve themselves just after waking, eating, drinking, and exercise.

△ **OUTDOOR RELIEF**
Teaching your puppy to relieve itself outside is vital in training it to be a responsible family member.

73 TOILET TRAINING OUTSIDE

Begin outdoor training for your puppy as soon as possible. Three-month-old puppies need to empty their bladders about every three or four hours. Take a small piece of soiled paper with you: the puppy will smell its own unique scent and be encouraged to transfer toileting outside. As it eliminates, say "Hurry up"; this will train your puppy to understand that it must relieve itself on that command.

74 CLEAN UP AFTER YOUR PUPPY

Always clean up after your puppy. Carry a pooper-scooper or a plastic bag with you when you take your dog for a walk, and place the mess in a provided dog bin. If you are in your yard, flush it down the toilet. Roundworms and other intestinal worms can be transmitted in dog feces, so worm your puppy regularly.

75 INTRODUCE THE LEASH

Begin training your puppy to accept a collar and leash as soon as you bring it home. Start by letting the puppy see and smell the collar. Avoiding eye contact, put the collar on, distracting it with words. Reward your puppy at this point. Actively play for a while, then remove the collar. Your puppy will soon learn to associate the collar with rewards. Once your puppy is content wearing its collar, kneel in front and attach the leash. Reward it for accepting the leash by giving it access to a toy.

▽ COLLARED!
If rewarded well, your puppy will accept a collar and leash.

76 MEETING A STRANGER

Arrange for a dog-loving friend to meet you and your puppy outdoors. Ask your friend to kneel down to greet the puppy, as this will help curb its inclination to jump up. Discourage direct eye contact, since this can provoke an unduly excited response, not uncommon in very young dogs. Finally, provide your friend with your puppy's favorite food treat as a reward for its behavior.

▽ A NEW FRIEND?
Your puppy should happily welcome approaches from strangers.

HEAD STROKE
Train your puppy to allow itself to be stroked by a stranger, even on its head, which is a gesture of dominance.

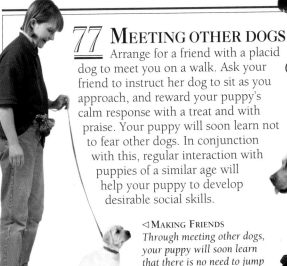

77 MEETING OTHER DOGS

Arrange for a friend with a placid dog to meet you on a walk. Ask your friend to instruct her dog to sit as you approach, and reward your puppy's calm response with a treat and with praise. Your puppy will soon learn not to fear other dogs. In conjunction with this, regular interaction with puppies of a similar age will help your puppy to develop desirable social skills.

◁ MAKING FRIENDS
Through meeting other dogs, your puppy will soon learn that there is no need to jump up on any animal that reminds it of its mother.

78 LEAVING YOUR PUPPY ALONE

No matter how much you enjoy being with your puppy, there will be many times when you must leave it on its own. Train your puppy to accept that this is part of its routine by confining it to its crate or pen. Then quietly walk away, signaling "Wait." Gradually accustom your puppy to being left alone for extended periods.

Hand signals "Wait"

LEFT ALONE ▷
When you leave your puppy alone for any length of time, remember to provide a bowl of fresh water and a toy for diversion.

NEXT STEPS

79 REPEAT THE COMMAND

Begin informal training as soon as you bring your new puppy home at eight weeks old. Whenever it does anything you want it to do on command, such as sit, say the appropriate word several times while the puppy maintains that position. Your puppy will rapidly learn to associate particular words with particular actions.

◁ SIT!
Your puppy will soon learn to sit on command.

Look your puppy in the eye

IMMEDIATE REBUKE
If your puppy does something you do not want it to, say "No!" but only as you catch it misbehaving. Never discipline a puppy after it has done something wrong, even seconds later. It will not associate your discipline with its action.

◁ CONSTANT PRAISE
Always praise your puppy when it does what you tell it to do. It will quickly learn what "good dog" means.

80 COME!

For safety and responsible control, your puppy must learn always to come to you on command. This is central to all obedience. Once your puppy has learned to accept a collar and leash, you can train your puppy with ease.

1 ▽ Put a collar and leash on your puppy. Kneel a short distance away, with the leash tucked securely under one knee. Hold a chewable or attractively scented toy as a reward.

Puppy is distracted and ignores owner

2 ▷ Call your puppy's name in a clear, friendly tone, to attract its attention. When it turns its head toward you, give the command "Come." Wave the toy as an enticement. Keep the leash slack; do not reel in your puppy, but encourage it to come willingly for the reward.

Speak to puppy in clear, warm tone

On command, puppy turns to look at toy

3 ▷ Welcome your puppy with open arms. Out of curiosity, it should walk toward you. As it moves, say "Good dog" in an enthusiastic voice. When the puppy reaches you, reward it with the toy. Never call your puppy to discipline it, or it will link returning to you with a reprimand.

Inviting gesture gets response from puppy

Intrigued puppy, eager to obey command

81 COME & SIT!

Training your puppy to come and sit is most important for the safety of your pet, for good relations with your family, friends, and in situations outside your home. Start this training early, and incorporate it into play sessions to ensure that your puppy always obeys you.

△ SIT!

1 ▽ Start training in a quiet, narrow space such as a hallway. Hold your puppy on a loose leash, call its name, and let it see that you have a food treat in your hand. As it starts to walk toward you, give the command "Come."

2 ◁ As your puppy reaches you, move the treat above its head. To keep its eye on the food, your puppy will naturally sit. As it does so, issue the command "Sit," and immediately give the reward. Repeat this simple exercise regularly before each meal, when your puppy will respond best to food incentives.

Praise puppy as it walks toward you

Puppy sits to keep an eye on treat

Offer reward calmly to avoid overexcitement

Keep leash slack, but pull on it gently to gain compliance if necessary

82 LIE DOWN!

By teaching your puppy to lie down, you are telling it who is in charge. Be firm during training, but remember to use lots of praise, as your puppy will respond well to verbal encouragement.

Keep your eyes fixed on puppy

Praise puppy when it lies down

Handle firmly but gently

1 △ Get your puppy in the sitting position and kneel down beside it. Command it to "Lie down," at the same time patting the ground in front of it.

2 △ If your puppy ignores your command, ease it to the ground by gently pressing on its body, at the same time pulling its front legs forward.

83 DOWN!

Kneel beside your seated puppy and hold its collar in one hand. With your other hand, place a treat by its nose. Move the treat down in an arc, drawing the puppy down as it follows the food with its nose. Still holding the collar, move the treat forward until your puppy is lying completely flat.

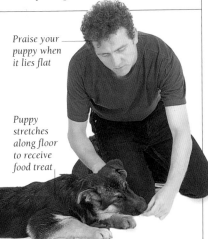

Praise your puppy when it lies flat

Puppy stretches along floor to receive food treat

LIE FLAT ▷
Command "Down" to make your puppy lie on the floor.

84 STAY!

Once your puppy is sitting comfortably, give the command "Stay." With the leash held loosely in your hand, and maintaining eye contact, get up and walk in front, repeating "Stay." Use a raised palm gesture rather than food rewards; your puppy will learn to recognize this gesture. Response to the "Stay" command is important in hazardous situations such as crossing a busy road.

Keep your palm slightly raised

Puppy listens to owner's voice

◁ SAFETY WARNING
Training your puppy to stay is essential for its safety outside.

85 JUMPING UP

If your puppy keeps jumping up, gently push it down and firmly say "No." Command it to sit, and then greet it. A puppy must be discouraged from this type of behavior early on, or it will keep up the bad habit for the rest of its life.

Learning not to jump up is a quick lesson

△ NO JUMPING
It might be endearing when your puppy jumps up to greet you, but you won't feel the same when it is fully grown.

Tail wags constantly with enthusiasm

86 CHEWING OBJECTS

When left on their own, some puppies will chew objects through frustration at being alone or to relieve boredom. Make sure you store away any personal objects your puppy might chew, such as shoes, clothes, or children's toys. Provide your pet with several dog toys, showering it with praise when it decides to chew them instead.

A GOOD DETERRENT
Your puppy will be attracted to many things in your home and will want to chew them all. Apply a nontoxic, bitter-tasting spray, available from most veterinary clinics – or sprinkle some lemon juice or pepper onto your shoes and other objects you want to protect, to act as a deterrent.

A GOOD CHEW ▷
Puppies like nothing better than to chew your slippers or shoes. Hide them away at all times.

87 TRAINING MORE THAN ONE PUPPY

Any training requires the undivided attention of both you and your puppy. If you have two or more puppies, train just one at a time, keeping the others out of sight and beyond hearing distance. Otherwise, those puppies may learn not to respond to your commands since their obedience is not being enforced.

ONE AT A TIME ▷
Play with your puppies together, but train them individually.

88 HEELING

Your puppy must always be under control when it is out walking with you, both for its own safety and as a courtesy to others. As a first step, train it indoors from an early age to walk to heel. You can then graduate to training it to accept a leash when it is ready. In this way, walking with your puppy will be a pleasure rather than an ordeal. Most puppies initially train best for heelwork off the leash, but some breeds, such as German Shepherds, respond best to walking on a leash from the start. Remember: lessons should always be enjoyable, so finish each training session with a game and a reward.

Puppy will follow food treat

Puppy smells potential reward

TRAIN & REWARD
Keep training lessons short: no more than 15 minutes a time up to four times a day. Be sure to reward your puppy with treats, and to praise it when it does well.

1 △ Kneel down beside your sitting puppy, firmly taking hold of its collar. Speak its name and, with your other, free hand, show it a tasty food treat to attract and keep its attention.

2 △ Hold the treat in front of the puppy's nose, and walk in a straight line while giving the command "Heel." The food scent will induce the puppy to follow. Keep your free hand low, ready to grasp the collar if the puppy tries to wander. When you stop walking, command "Wait."

Keep hand free to grasp collar if necessary

Puppy turns to follow treat

As you move treat, puppy follows

3 △ Keep the treat low to prevent your puppy from jumping up. Bend your knees and then turn right, drawing the food around you as you move. Repeat the command "Heel." Your puppy will immediately speed up to walk around you in order to keep up with the treat.

4 △ With your puppy still to your left, command it to be "Steady." Place the treat near your puppy's mouth, then move it to the left. The puppy will then follow. Train your puppy regularly, but only for a few minutes at a time. End each training session with a treat.

◁ WALK TO HEEL
Training your puppy indoors to walk to heel is the perfect preparation for training it outdoors to walk with a collar and leash. When it learns to heel, your outdoor excursions together will be a pleasure, not a pain!

89 WALKING ON THE LEASH

Look down at puppy

Once your puppy has mastered the skill of heeling without a leash, you can begin to train it to walk to heel with a leash and collar. Use a long training leash for this task, and choose a time when your puppy is relaxed but alert. Train it in a quiet area in- or outdoors, and do not lose patience. Lessons should always be enjoyable. Finish every training session with a game, and don't forget to praise your puppy when it behaves well.

Puppy looks up expectantly

Keep looking down at puppy

Turn your body around to the left

Pull gently on leash if puppy walks ahead

1 △ Stand to the right of your puppy and hold the training leash and a food treat with your right hand. Pick up the slack of the leash with your left hand. Get your puppy's attention and command it to "Sit."

2 ◁ Swing your body around on your right foot by moving your left foot in front of you. Look down at your puppy and give the command "Heel." If your puppy walks too far ahead, give the leash a gentle tug with your left hand.

3 ◁With your puppy beside you in the heel position, offer it a reward. Praise it with the words "Good puppy." Repeat the command "Sit." Praise it again when it obeys.

Puppy turns to follow treat

Puppy sits obediently by your heel

WHEN TO STOP
If your puppy does not respond properly to your commands during training, stop the session with a command you know it will obey. Praise it for obeying you.

4 △After teaching your puppy to walk in a straight line to the "Heel" command, teach it to turn to the right by guiding it with the food treat. Train a puppy only for a short period of time to keep its attention.

Puppy concentrates on food as it's moved in front of nose

5 ▷ Once the right turn has been mastered, begin left-turn training. Hold the treat above the puppy's nose. Keep the puppy close as you turn to the left, controlling it with the leash. Command "Steady."

HEALTH & SAFETY

90 VACCINATE YOUR PUPPY

Take your puppy to the vet to get it vaccinated against a range of infectious diseases. For additional protection, your vet might advise avoiding unfamiliar dogs for a few weeks. Contact with known healthy dogs should continue, however, to ensure that your puppy becomes properly socialized.

VET CHECK ▷
Your vet will check your puppy carefully to make sure it is fit and well.

91 BASIC FIRST AID KIT

The principles of human first aid apply also to dogs. Your aims are to preserve life, prevent further injury, minimize pain, promote healing, and get your puppy safely to a vet for help. Have a fully stocked first aid kit handy, and use it to treat minor wounds. Keep all medicines out of the reach of children and pets.

△ SCISSORS

△ COTTON BALLS

△ DISINFECTANT

△ GAUZE

△ TAPE

STRONG CARRYING BOX ▷

92 BASIC BANDAGING

If your puppy is bleeding from an accident, remove it from risk of further injury. Clean and bandage the wound to prevent any more damage until you can get to a vet. Bandaging will prevent further blood loss and shock. Spurting blood from a severed artery needs urgent medical attention. Slower bleeding from a vein can be stopped by applying pressure with an absorbent pad and a bandage.

1 △ While someone contacts a vet, apply a gauze pad soaked in cold water to the wound. Do not use cotton as it will leave fibers in the wound.

2 △ If the bleeding does not stop, or to prevent it starting again, cover the area with a lint-free absorbent pad and secure it with a bandage.

Wrap tail in bandage

◁ BANDAGING A TAIL
Disinfect the wound and apply a lint-free absorbent pad. Start at the tip and bandage up the tail toward the body.

BANDAGING A TAIL TO THE BODY ▷
If your puppy's tail is long enough, bandage it to the body to prevent it wagging. Do not bandage too tightly.

93 GIVING LIQUID MEDICINES

To give a liquid medicine to your puppy, use a syringe obtained from your vet or from a drugstore. Squirt the medicine into the mouth, not down the throat where it may enter the windpipe. Hold your puppy's muzzle until it swallows.

Aim into mouth, not down throat

LIQUID RELIEF ▷
You can give your puppy cough syrup and other liquids through a syringe.

Pill can be hidden in favorite food

94 SWALLOWING PILLS

To give your puppy a pill or other solid form of medicine, command your puppy to sit down. Open its mouth and then insert the pill as far back in the mouth as possible. Then gently hold the jaw shut and tilt its head upward. Stroke the neck to induce your puppy to swallow. This may take a few seconds.

TAKING THE PILL ▷
You will need to be firm but patient when giving your puppy a pill.

95 PREVENT ROAD ACCIDENTS

Many traffic accidents could be prevented by proper obedience training. Make sure that your puppy is well trained and always under the control of a responsible person when walking outside, especially near a busy road. If an accident occurs, do not panic. Use your common sense. If your puppy has been injured, and is still at risk from further injury, remove it from the source of danger. Muzzle it with a scarf or tie to stop it from biting you out of shock or pain.

96 HOW TO REMOVE FOREIGN OBJECTS

Your puppy is likely to get something stuck in its mouth at some time or another. Train your puppy not to chew dangerous objects, as it can choke on bone splinters or twigs. Small balls and toys are also easily swallowed. Dislodge these with the handle of a spoon or cooking tongs as soon as possible to let your puppy breathe.

1 △ To remove twigs or bone splinters lodged between the upper teeth or in the back of the throat, restrain your puppy firmly. Open its mouth wide.

2 △ Hold the mouth open and remove the object using round-ended metal tweezers or a pair of pliers. Do not use your fingers — you may get bitten.

97 HYPOTHERMIA

Hypothermia is most likely to occur in puppies that have been in freezing water even for just a few minutes, especially those without thick hair. Vigorously rub the puppy with a towel to dry it, then wrap in a warm blanket. Keep it warm, but avoid overheating.

△ WRAPPED IN A BLANKET

98 CHEMICAL HAZARDS

Chewing is a favorite pastime for all puppies, so keep all household, garage, garden, and swimming-pool chemicals stored safely out of sight and reach. Never give your puppy an empty chemical container as a toy, because it will not be able to tell the difference between this and a harmful one, with potentially lethal results.

△ **DANGEROUS TOY**
Always provide your puppy with safe toys to chew, not empty chemical containers.

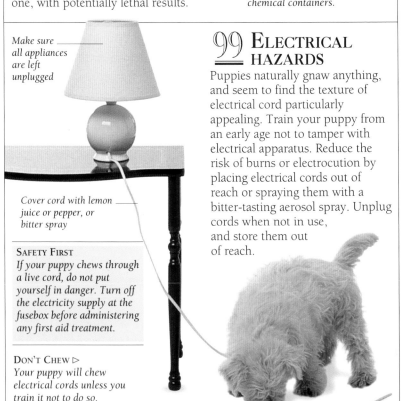

Make sure all appliances are left unplugged

Cover cord with lemon juice or pepper, or bitter spray

SAFETY FIRST
If your puppy chews through a live cord, do not put yourself in danger. Turn off the electricity supply at the fusebox before administering any first aid treatment.

DON'T CHEW ▷
Your puppy will chew electrical cords unless you train it not to do so.

99 ELECTRICAL HAZARDS

Puppies naturally gnaw anything, and seem to find the texture of electrical cord particularly appealing. Train your puppy from an early age not to tamper with electrical apparatus. Reduce the risk of burns or electrocution by placing electrical cords out of reach or spraying them with a bitter-tasting aerosol spray. Unplug cords when not in use, and store them out of reach.

100 AVOID HEATSTROKE

Puppies cannot lose heat by sweating since they have few sweat glands. All they can do is pant. Heatstroke is one of the most common causes of avoidable death in dogs. Remember: in the presence of heat and inadequate ventilation, a puppy's temperature rapidly rises to 110°F (43°C). A hot car is a deathtrap: do not leave your puppy in a hot car at any time of the year, even for a few minutes.

101 IN THE CAR

Take your puppy on frequent short trips to get it used to the car. Avoid feeding it before a journey, and cover the upholstery and floor with newspapers or towels in case of an accident. Always carry fresh water to quench its thirst, and stop for exercise every couple of hours.

Crate fits well into rear of car

△ CARRYING BOX
Buy a specially-made pet carrier for trips away with your puppy. The box has a carrying handle, locking catch, ventilation slits, and room inside for a comfortable journey.

◁ CAR TRAVEL
You may prefer to transport your puppy in its crate, providing it fits into your car. Alternatively, install a safety grille to restrict your puppy to the rear of the car.

BELT UP YOUR PUPPY
If you cannot install a grille in your car, or have no room for a crate or carrying box, install dog seatbelts in the back seat, or tie its leash to the seatbelt anchors.

INDEX

A

accidents, 66
adult dogs, 11, 26, 53
age of puppy, 18
American Water Spaniel, 9
anal region, 21
animal shelters, 17

B

balanced diet, 31
bandaging, 65
baskets, 24
bathing, 46-7
beanbags, 24
beds, 24
begging, 34
Bergamasco, 9
Bernese Mountain Dog, 9
biscuits, 37
bitches, 10, 18
bleeding, 65
bottle feeding, 13
bowls, 35
Boxer, 20, 21
breeders, 17, 18
brushes, 42
buying puppies, 17-22

C

Cairn Terrier, 32
calcium, 41
canned foods, 35, 36
car travel, 69
carbohydrates, 31, 37
carrying boxes, 23, 69
cats, 26
chemical hazards, 68

chewing, 59
chews, 38
chicken, 40
children, 25
choke chains, 28
choking, 67
choosing a puppy, 8-12,
  19-21
coat:
  choosing a puppy, 12
  color, 15
  grooming, 42-7
collars, 28, 52
combs, 42
"Come!" training, 55, 56
commands, training, 54
crates, 24, 53, 69
crossbreeds, 11
curly coats, 12

D-E

dens, 24, 27
diet, see feeding
discipline, 50, 54
diseases, vaccination, 15,
  64
distemper, 15
"Down!" training, 57
dry dog meal, 36
dry foods, 36
ears, 21, 45
eggs, 39
electrical hazards, 68
equipment:
  feeding, 35
  grooming, 42
eyes, 21, 45

F

fat, in diet, 31
feces, cleaning up, 51
feeding puppies, 13, 16,
  31-41
feet, 21
female dogs, 10, 18
first aid kit, 64
first night at home, 27
fish, 40
fresh foods, 39, 40

G

German Shepherd, 19, 32,
  60
Great Dane, 32
grooming, 42-7
gums, 21, 45

H

halters, 28
handling puppies, 15
harnesses, 28
Harrier, 12
health, 64-9
health certificates, 20, 22
heart, 39
heatstroke, 69
heeling, 60-1
hygiene, feeding, 35
hypothermia, 67

I-J-K

ID tags, 25, 26
identification, 26
illness, special meals, 40
jumping up, 58

kennels, 30
Kerry Blue Terrier, 12
King Charles Spaniel, 8

L

Labrador Retriever, 8
leashes, 28, 52
  walking on, 62-3
leaving puppies alone, 53
legs, 21
"Lie down!" training, 57
liquid medicines, 66
litters, 13-14, 19
liver, 39
long coats, 12, 44

M-N

male puppies, 10
meat, 31, 35, 39, 40
medicines, 66
Mexican Toy Hairless, 8
microchips, 26
milk, newborn pups, 13
minerals, 41
mongrels, 10
mouth, 21
muzzles, 22
nails, clipping, 45
names, 25, 48
newborn puppies, 13-16
"No" training, 50, 54

O-P

obedience training, 15,
  54-63
Old English Sheepdog, 12
paper, toilet training, 51
parasites, 47
parvovirus, 15
pasta, 39
pedigree dogs, 10
pens, 24, 53

pet carrier, 23, 69
pet shops, 17
pills, swallowing, 66
plants, poisonous, 30
poisons, 30, 68
pooper-scoopers, 51
praise, 49, 54
protein, 31
puppy farms, 17, 18

R

regulations, local, 22
rewards, 49
rice, 40
road accidents, 66
Rough Collie, 12
roundworms, 51

S

semimoist foods, 37
sex, choosing puppies, 10
shampoo, 46-7
short coats, 12, 43
silky coats, 44
"Sit!" training, 56
skin care, 47
smooth coats, 12, 43
socialization, 14, 50
Springer Spaniel, 32
"Stay!" training, 58
strangers, meeting, 52
stroking, 52

T

tails, bandaging, 65
teeth, 21
  chews, 38
  cleaning, 45
temperature, food, 34
toilet training, 51
toxic plants, 30
toys, 29
training, 15, 48-63
treats, 38, 49

V-W-Y

vaccination, 15, 64
vegetables, 39, 41
vegetarian food, 41
vets, 22, 64
vitamins, 31, 41
walking, training, 60-3
water, drinking, 35
weaning, 16
weight gain, 14
worms, 51
wounds, 65
yards, 30
Yorkshire Terrier, 32

ACKNOWLEDGMENTS

DK Publishing would like to thank Hilary Bird for compiling the index, Ann Kay for proofreading, Mark Bracey for computer assistance, Holly Shackleton for animal handling, and Jane Bailey, Sue Dunning, Hazel Ridgwell, and Sue Seath for letting their puppies be photographed.

Photography
KEY: t *top*, b *bottom*, c *center*
All photographs by Tracy Morgan, assisted by Stella Smyth-Carpenter, and by Andy Crawford, Steve Gorton, and Tim Ridley, except: Paul Bricknell 2, 11t; Jane Burton 1, 5, 10b, 59t; Dave King 50b; Steve Shott 3, 23, 25, 45, 64b, 71; David Ward 26t, 41c; Jerry Young 10t.

Illustration
Jane Pickering 30.